Liverpool Docks

FOUR DECADES OF CHANGE

PHILIP PARKER

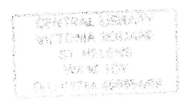

TEMPUS

Acknowledgements

Firstly thanks to Elaine for her support and to Kerry and Lucy who have 'suffered' numerous diversions via 'The Dock Road' to see which vessels are in dock.

I would also like to thank friends, family and colleagues at ACL and Mersey Docks who have helped and assisted with the contents of this book and with support in making photographic choices.

First published 2004

Tempus Publishing Ltd
The Mill, Brimscombe Port
Stroud, Gloucestershire GL5 2QG
www.tempus-publishing.com

British Library Cataloguing in Publication Data.
A catalogue record for this book is available from the British Library.

ISBN 0 7524 3086 6

Typesetting and origination by Tempus Publishing.
Printed and bound in Great Britain.

Contents

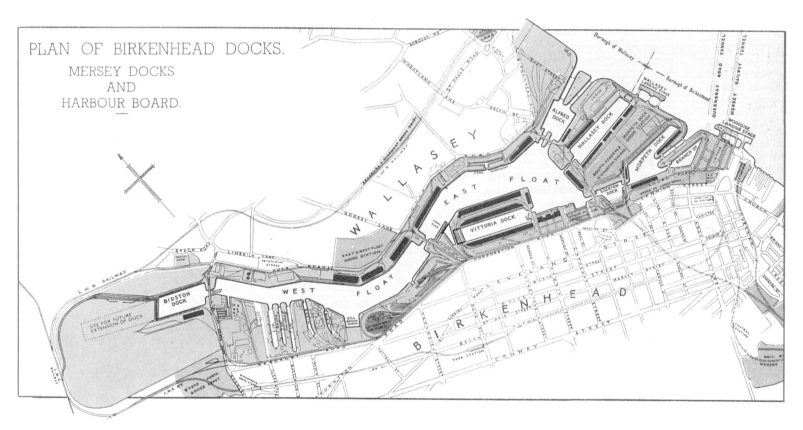

Mersey Docks and Harbour Board plan of Birkenhead in 1958.

CHAPTER ONE

The Port at Work in the 1960s

The year 1965 saw the publication of the Devlin Report into UK port workings. Previously, stevedoring companies operated within the Port hiring labour on a casual basis for discharging and loading cargo from vessels as well as for the handling of cargo on the Port's quaysides. The report recommended that the number of companies should be reduced and the Port Authority should employ a workforce from within the structure of the National Dock Labour Board.

The Mersey Docks and Harbour Board (MDHB) set up the cargo handling division based at West Langton Dock, an area previously refurbished as part of the Langton-Canada Dock Improvement Scheme across the west side of Langton, Brocklebank and Canada Docks.

The master porter and stevedore operators now had appropriated berths for regular trades, with ships having designated places to discharge and load their cargoes.

In 1966, for the second year in succession, an all-time record was established for trade within the Port. The total imports and exports had risen to 29,726,715 tons, a rise of 4.8 per cent compared with the previous year and 18.6 per cent higher than in 1964. The year's trade had been affected by many factors, including government restrictions on imports and the National Seamen's dispute, so the Port's fortunes were clearly improving.

Several major improvements were undertaken at this time, beginning with royal assent being granted to the Bill for the proposed works at Seaforth, which had been designed to keep pace with the developing container trade.

Several other Port modernisation projects included South Vittoria Dock for Blue Funnel Export Ships; a roll-on, roll-off berth at South West Princes Dock for sailings to Belfast; a dedicated timber berth at North 3 Canada Dock with four 10-ton quayside cranes; the development of North 2 Alexandra Dock, a new transit shed with specialised equipment for handling refrigerated foodstuffs and new transit sheds in the South Dock system at Queens, Kings and East Harrington Docks, primarily for the fruit trade. The river channels were also deepened to 28ft at low water to take larger vessels including oil tankers, and the Bar Channel was re-aligned.

Labour at the time was provided by the National Dock Labour Board (NDLB) with a work force of 14,000 at the start of the year. Dockworkers employed by the NDLB reported for work before the normal start time of 8a.m. and 1p.m. to seek work.

Stevedore operators requiring labour to work vessels would order men from the local control, adjacent to the ship or handling operation. Labour controls were numbered from one upwards, box 1 being Gladstone two north, box 2 Gladstone one south, etc. Known locally as the 'pen', dockworkers would be assigned to either a ship's hatch or a quay operation until that job was completed, when they would return to the pen for further hire. The labour force was split into various categories. While some men had dual skills, in general the main areas of employment were: holdsmen (ship); porters (quay); deckhands for operating ships' gear, winches and derricks; and roof-crane drivers for the electric quayside cranes capable of moving along

PORT OF

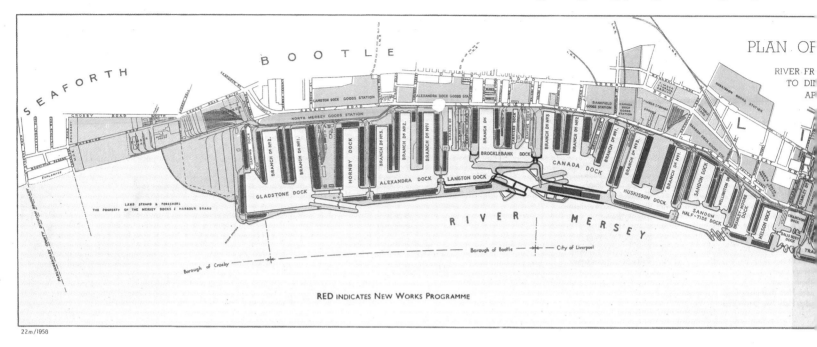

PLAN OF

RIVER FR
TO DI
AP

RED INDICATES NEW WORKS PROGRAMME

22m/1958

Mersey Docks and Harbour Board plan of the Port of Liverpool in 1958.

rails on the quayside (drawing the power supply from either a roof rail or a ground socket). Forklift truck drivers, bogie drivers and mobile-crane drivers on the quay positioned cargo for loading or for delivery to road transport.

Each 'gang' would have a 'hatch boss' who would assist and oversee the hatch they were discharging or loading. In turn these men would be supervised by foremen on both the ship and the quay. Most stevedoring companies employed superintendents who would be the link between the ship's owner, the ship's command and the workforce.

The basic hours of work were from 8a.m. to 12 noon and from 1p.m. to 5p.m. Monday to Friday, making up a forty hour working week. Overtime, if required to maintain a ship's schedule, was in the main on a daily basis between 5p.m. and

7p.m. If a particular hatch was not moving at the same speed as the others, overtime could be used, but Saturday morning working had disappeared during the early 1960s, leaving Sunday as the main extra working day. The hours on Sundays would be 8a.m. to 11a.m. and 1p.m. to 4p.m. The additional hour at midday was for men attending church, and the afternoon period would be taken without a break. Night work was available but rarely used, unless there was a surplus of labour and the ship owner had a deadline to meet.

Conditions and facilities had not improved much since the period after the Second World War. However, parts of the Devlin Report recommended improvements and these improvements started to appear in the mid-1960s. They included wash rooms, ablution blocks with hot running water and drying facilities, as

LIVERPOOL

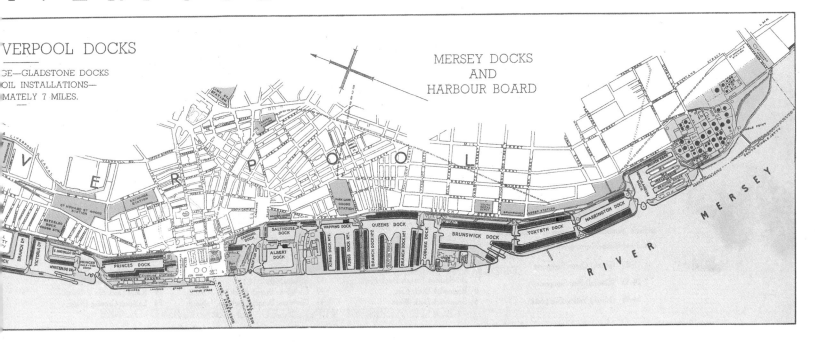

IVERPOOL DOCKS

GE—GLADSTONE DOCKS
OIL INSTALLATIONS—
MATELY 7 MILES.

MERSEY DOCKS
AND
HARBOUR BOARD

well as canteens providing hot drinks and meals. The MDHB spent £350,000 on these amenities in 1966 alone.

Decasualisation came into effect in September 1967 (after a six-week strike over its implementation) when registered dockworkers (RDWs) were allocated to specific stevedoring companies while still under the National Dock Labour Board (NDLB). This caused several of the smaller operators within the Port to review their operations, and by the end of 1968 three of them (Scruttons, Freight Conveyors and Mersey Ports Stevedoring) had approached the MDHB with a view to taking over their operations and subsequent workforces. By 1969 the MDHB employed one fifth of the dock labour within the Port of Liverpool.

To cope with the demands of a busy port, the MDHB set up a Port Information Centre designed to assist haulage companies

and to prevent vehicles from spending hours waiting on the dock estate to be tipped or loaded.

Based in the Port of Liverpool building at Liverpool's Pier Head, the Centre received information by radio patrols on thirty-seven miles of quay in order to give up-to-the-minute details of quayside conditions for the Port's customers.

The southern stretch of docklands from Pier Head to Herculaneum had a mixture of modernised berths and the no longer viable docks and warehouses centred round the Albert Dock. Valuable land in the heart of the City's waterfront, these warehouses and narrow quays had outlived their usefulness for modern port work and the MDHB looked for a suitable buyer in order that proceeds could be used to lessen the cost of the Seaforth works.

The original plan for Seaforth included an additional river entrance. This idea was shelved, however, and Gladstone Lock was used as Seaforth's river entrance instead. This decision reduced the cost of the installation but greatly increased the dock tonnage capacity and the potential completion date.

Most of the Liverpool and Birkenhead dock estate had railway connections fed from local goods stations by a mixture of British Railways' locomotives and MDHB diesel engines. On the opposite side of Regent Road (known locally as 'the Dock Road'), British Railways had major goods depots at strategic points for the transfer of cargo to and from the quaysides.

The modern quaysides had electric, roof rail-mounted cranes to handle cargo in and out of the ships' hatches. These normally had a limited lifting capacity of three and five tons. For greater lifting capacity the MDHB had a fleet of steam-powered floating cranes of up to 200 tons: *Mammoth* (capacity 200 tons), *Atlas* (capacity 100 tons), *Samson* (capacity 60 tons), *Birket* (capacity 60 tons), *Fender* (capacity 60 tons) and *Titan* (capacity 25 tons).

United States Lines vessel American Importer *is seen here at North 2 Gladstone Dock, May 1966. Built in 1946, the vessel weighed 8,228 gross registered tons, had a length of 459ft, a beam of 63ft and was capable of 16 knots service speed. Powered by steam turbines, this type of vessel traded between the east coast of North America and Europe. Astern of her are two tugs in the colours of The Alexandra Towing Company. Also visible is a Federal Boat on West Gladstone Dock, the main loading berth for Australia and New Zealand.*

As a result of a British Seaman's Dispute, the summer of 1966 saw the Port of Liverpool accomodate its most vessels at any one time.

Gladstone Dock No.1, the North Side, was the regular berth for Canadian Pacific's Empress of Canada *and* Empress of England, *which were both freighters and passenger liners. After discharging passengers at Princes Landing Stage at Pier Head, the ships moved back to Gladstone for the discharge and loading of cargo before returning to the Landing Stage for westbound passengers for the Atlantic crossing between UK and Canada.*

A typical look within the Port at this time would see ships of Blue Funnel Line in S.1 Gladstone Dock, Canadian Pacific on the opposite side, United States Lines ships on the North Side of No.2, and the south side being occupied by ships trading with Australia and New Zealand. These would have included Blue Funnel, Port Line and Shaw Savill to name but three.

Above: *South West One Gladstone Dock, Blue Funnel Line's* Polyphemus *alongside, one of the fleet of modern general cargo vessels built in the late 1950s for trade between Europe, the Far East and Australia.*

Below: *Clan Line vessel* Clan Graham *pictured turning into No.2 Gladstone Branch Dock assisted by tugs from the Liverpool Screw Towing & Lighterage Co. (known as 'Cock' Tugs).*

Gladstone Graving Dock was used by many of the Shipping Companies with major bases in Liverpool. Between Gladstone and Alexandra docks is Hornby Dock, used in a variety of trades for Furness Withy, Ellerman & Papayanni Lines, Saguenay Shipping Company and other trades.

Vessels docking in Alexandra Dock also accessed from Gladstone Dock using the Gladstone Lock that opened in 1927. This was and still is the largest impounding lock within the Port.
The Shipping Companies of Blue Star, Lamport & Holt, Ellerman Hall Line and several others had appropriated berths within the three branch docks and the west side of Alexandra Dock.

Above: *Blue Star Line vessel* Newcastle Star *berthed at Hornby Dock. The tug in the foreground is from The Alexandra Towing Company Fleet.*

Below: *Clan Line vessel* Clan MacLachlan *passing through Hornby to Alexandra Dock. Also visible on the north side of Hornby Dock is an unnamed Lamport & Holt Line Ship. Note the MDHB dock gate staff on duty when ships pass through from dock to dock.*

Top: *Alexandra Branch Dock No.1 with Furness Prince Line's* Norman Prince *on the north side and Ellerman & Papayanni Line's* Crosbian. *Prince Line traded between Europe and Canada with calls at various North America Ports. Ellerman & Papayanni Line traded the short sea routes of the Mediterranean region.*

Middle: *Langton Branch Dock with four Ellerman ships tied up. This dock has since been filled in along with the Langton Graving Docks. The transit shed on the left side is still standing and is now used for bulk cargo.*

Bottom: *Two of the mail boats,* Accra *and* Apapa, *berthed alongside North Brocklebank Dock.* Accra *was built in 1947, with* Apapa *built the following year. The boats were similar in size at 11,650 gross tons, with an overall length of 471ft and a beam of 66ft. Powered by diesel engines, these twin-screw vessels had a service speed of 16 knots.*

The berths at West Langton Dock were under the control of MDHB Cargo Handling with an administration base on West Langton and equipment base (gear store) alongside Langton Lock. These berths had wider quaysides between the ship and the transit shed, thus allowing for heavier pieces of cargo as well as unit loads and palletisation so as to improve speed of handling and reduce cargo damage.

The Langton-Canada Improvement Scheme was the largest major dock programme carried out in this country since the Second World War, with the entrance and lock gates officially opened by HM Queen Elizabeth II on 14 December 1962.

Two-storey warehouses were built alongside the west sides of both Canada and Huskisson Docks as part of this scheme, West Brocklebank, having a single storey transit shed and a large storage area behind for timber cargoes from the Far East, discharged from Ben Line and Blue Funnel Line Ships.

After relocating from the southern dock system, Elder Dempster Lines occupied the North Brocklebank Branch Dock for both cargo and passenger ships. The three 'mail' boats, as they were known – *Aureol, Accra* and *Apapa*, used the Princes Landing Stage in a way similar to Canadian Pacific. They ran a weekly service to West Africa.

Situated between Brocklebank Branch Dock and Brocklebank Graving Dock was Carriers Dock, used in the late 1960s for the B&I Line Car Ferry Service between Liverpool and Dublin before it relocated to Waterloo Dock. Carriers Dock was also used during the 1970s by Booker Line.

After use by the MDHC as a marine base, the sheds were finally demolished along with the infilling of Brocklebank Graving Dock in 1984-85. This was to be the site for Bibby's, and was later to become a major industrial complex for American producer Cargill.

The refurbished Canada Dock had three branch docks with transit sheds on most quays. North 3 Canada was to be the first specialist timber terminal, while on the south side vessels of the Strick Line loaded general cargo for the Persian Gulf.

Branch Dock No.2 was the base for T&J Harrison. Up to four vessels could be seen at any one time handling cargo for a variety of destinations, including the West Indies and South and East Africa, while on the opposite side, MacAndrew's short sea ships traded with ports of the Iberian Peninsula.

The West side berths of Canada and Huskisson handled a variety of trades, predominantly discharging cargoes for numerous shipping companies.

Huskisson Dock was built similar in size to Canada Dock, but due to the blitz of May 1941 the middle Branch Dock No.2 was completely filled in. On the night of 3-4 May 1941 a fire and explosions on board the T&J Brocklebank cargo ship *Malakand*, which had in excess of 1,000 tons of shells and bombs aboard, left a trail of destruction over acres of dock space. The site is still known as the *Malakand* site.

No.1 Branch Dock was the main berth for Cunard Line's cargo vessels along with the last of the passenger ships.

Right: *Two views of Cunard Line's ships at Huskisson Dock. On the north side is the freighter* Samaria *and on the south side the passenger liner* Carinthia. *Built in 1965,* Samaria *weighed 5,837 gross tons, had a length of 457ft, a beam of 60ft and was powered by a diesel engine giving a service speed of 17.5 knots. This vessel traded between Liverpool or Southampton and North America, the Gulf Ports and Canada. In the winter months ships called at Halifax (Nova Scotia), Quebec and Montreal being the summer ports of call.*

The Carinthia *was built in 1956, weighed 21,947 gross tons, had a length of 608ft, a beam of 80ft and was powered by twin-screw steam turbines giving a service speed of 20 knots. This vessel operated the passenger service between Liverpool and New York and Halifax, Nova Scotia.*

Left: *The Cunard freighter* Alaunia *berthed at the North East No.1 Dock. Built in 1960, it weighed 7,004 gross tons, had a length of 490ft, a beam of 63ft and was powered by steam turbines giving a service speed of 17.5 knots.*

Beyond Huskisson Dock is Sandon Dock, appropriated to Head Line in the 1960s for the services to Canada, calling at Halifax, Montreal and Quebec.

Left below: *The Port of Birkenhead also played a prominent part within the Port, and several major shipping companies had allocated berths on this side of the river with the dock system accessed from Alfred Lock between the ferry stations of Woodside and Seacombe.*

An unnamed ship from the City Line waits for high water to enter the lock. Also in the picture is the Mersey Ferry Leasowe.

Below: *Vittoria Dock, Birkenhead, was the main loading berth for Blue Funnel Line vessels. Pictured in the middle berth is* Peleus *with another Blue Funnel ship ahead; two of the Mersey Docks floating cranes are also pictured.*

A view of Cammel Laird's dry dock, with a vessel of the Royal Fleet Auxiliary undergoing repairs. A second vessel under repair to the north is from the Isle of Man Steam Packet Company.

Above: *Looking towards the Vittoria Dock complex, still awaiting completion of the Blue Funnel transit shed. Pictured are vessels from Blue Funnel, Clan and Brocklebank Lines.*

Above right: *Viewed from the Birkenhead side, looking at the Princes Landing Stage. Alongside is the Isle of Man Steam Packet vessel Manx Maid built in the early 1960s for the increasing passenger trade with the Island. This vessel also carried passenger cars. Also pictured is a Royal Navy frigate F28 HMS Cleopatra and a collection of tugs. Riverside Station is also visible behind Manx Maid.*

Right: *Princes Landing Stage viewed from the North.*

Above and right: *Tug boats of the period. Here two of the Rea Towing Company fleet,* Throstlegarth *and* Bangarth, *are pictured in the south dock system at Harrington Dock. The vessels in the background were typical of the type and size using the south docks.*

Below: *West Gladstone dock in 1967 with the T&J Brocklebank general cargo vessel* Mawana *pictured discharging cargo from the after hatches. Built in 1958 with a gross tonnage of 8,744, a length of 150m and a beam of 19m, it was powered by steam turbines giving a service speed of 16.5 knots with single-screw propulsion.*

One of the well-known companies of the day, Mawana's owners operated several vessels on a variety of routes from the UK and Europe including India, Pakistan, Ceylon and the Gulf ports and the east coast of the United States of America.

Above, opposite and overleaf: *In September 1969 the famous railway locomotive A3 Pacific Class 4-6-2* Flying Scotsman *was shipped to America on a Cunard Line freighter* Saxonia *5,149 gross tons. This selection of* pictures shows several spectators on the Dock Road watching the MDHB floating crane Mammoth lifting the locomotive body from the rails adjacent to the dock wall to the prepared position on the freighter's starboard side.

The specialist lifting beam was supplied courtesy of A.E. Smith Coggins stevedores in the Port. The engine would be positioned on rails fixed to heavy timbers and secured with wires for the sea passage across the North Atlantic.

In the background is the MDHB Brocklebank warehouse.
(Photographs courtesy Cunard-Brocklebank)

CHAPTER TWO

Gladstone Container Terminal

Originally built as a graving dock in 1913 with its own river entrance, this dock became part of Gladstone Dock in 1927. The dock was accessed from Gladstone river entrance to the south of No.1 Branch Dock. After a successful period as a graving dock, its use was changed to that of a container terminal in the summer of 1968.

With limited resources, office accommodation consisted of an ex-Liverpool Corporation double-decker bus. The 50-ton capacity graving dock crane on the south side, fitted with a container spreader, lifted the first containers on and off the Ellerman-chartered *Estremadurian*. This was a small German flag coaster converted to take containers three high under deck and single height on deck, and which traded between Liverpool and Oporto and Leixoes in Portugal. Packing and unpacking of the containers took place some distance away at East Hornby Dock. Quayside container handling was by Lancer Boss side loaders used for containers on the general cargo berths and early Clark six-wheeled straddle carriers.

As the container revolution gathered pace the following year, the MDHB invested in two ship-to-shore container cranes, built by Stothert & Pitt of Bath, located on the north side with the stacking area directly behind. Additional straddle carriers were purchased to give a fleet of six. Running from north to south was a transit shed used for packing and unpacking containers.

Several major shipping companies with great traditions in general cargo moved into the world of containers. United States Lines operated with converted general cargo vessels such

as *American Rover* and *Resolute*, until these were replaced by new tonnages of the *American Lancer/Lark/Liberty* Class. Cunard Line, which were part of the consortium of ACL (Atlantic Container Lines) along with other major European companies including Holland America Line, Wallenius Lines, Swedish America, Transatlantic and CGT of France, operated a fleet of new roll on, roll off container vessels. These included Cunard's *Atlantic Conveyor*, one of the second generation of container vessels. Blue Star Line formed part of the consortium with Johnson Line of Sweden and the East Asiatic Company of Denmark to form Johnson Scan Star. Canadian Pacific, in partnership with Head Donaldson Line, operated a service to Canada from Gladstone, with purpose-built cont-ainer ships, including chartered tonnages and Head Line's *Inishowen Head*.

During 1969 when one of their vessels, the *Manchester Courage*, had a mishap with a lock gate on the Manchester Ship Canal, Manchester Liners transferred operations to Liverpool on a temporary basis. Later the same year saw the start of ACL's Liverpool service. The area known as North Mersey Goods Yard, running from north to south adjacent to Regent Road between Gladstone Gate and Strand Road (the yard previously used for rail haulage), was levelled to form an export car compound with cars driven directly on board the new generation of transatlantic carriers. Left-hand-drive vehicles for the American market included Triumph Spitfires, TR 4/5/6s, Jaguar E Types and the Austin America, known in the UK as the 1100 or 1300.

As the bigger operators used Gladstone, the smaller short sea operators, such as Ellerman Line, Mac Andrews, Zim Line and Moss Hutchinson, used the reclaimed North Hornby Dock equiped with a 35-ton capacity crane and a fleet of side loaders.

These modern advances took place within feet of the building of the Seaforth Dock complex. MDHB were early pioneers in the world of computers at Gladstone, which was a forerunner to future computer control at Seaforth.

The hours of work demanded by these new 'consortiums' and the need to keep the berth free for the next vessel was paramount. Day work started earlier subject to the vessels' arrival time and the time taken to tie up after locking in at Gladstone Lock. Night work became a regular feature with most of the ships working around the clock to finish in time to catch the first available lock on the next tide. Often men would work in excess of fourteen hours on a container vessel, most of which had been converted from general cargo and often required container lashings in the holds after containers had been loaded.

The modern purpose-built container carriers of US Lines/ACL/Johnson Scan Star and CP Ships had cellular hatches covered by watertight hatch covers lifted on and off by the container cranes. Inside the hatches the containers would fit in exact slots for either 20ft or 40ft containers. When a mixture of 20ft or 40ft containers was stowed, stacking cones or twist locks would be placed in the corner castings of each container to hold them in position during the voyage. On the hatch tops the same type of gear would be positioned to hold the containers with lashings in various forms at the forward and after ends of the containers depending on the stack height.

In the last months of Gladstone, the MDHB introduced a three shift working pattern in all cargo handling areas. The hours of work were: day work 8a.m. to 12 noon and 1p.m. to 5p.m., evening work 5p.m. to 11p.m. and night work 11p.m. to 6a.m. However, the night shift was more applicable to the container terminals.

The end of the 1960s and the early 1970s were years of financial crisis for the Port, which came as near to closure as at any time in its history. The MDHB struggled to come to terms with technological changes and move forward with the new era of shipping. With the Board unable to meets its debts, a Bill was put before Parliament to make the Port Authority a statutory company, and in 1971 the passing of the Mersey Docks & Harbour Act changed the former Board to The Mersey Docks & Harbour Co. (MDHC).

Opposite above: *The construction of the first container crane in Liverpool. Pictured from the south side of Gladstone graving dock, the MDHB floating crane* Mammoth *is positioning the crane's boom. When in use the boom is lowered over the span of the vessel, and when not in use the boom is raised against the A frame on the top of the structure. The locking mechanism of 'boom latches' is visible on the top cross centre beam. Access for driving was by means of cross-beam ladder visible on the west side of the crane. The small cabin under the crane's housing is the boom operating station.*

Opposite below: *Built in 1969 for the developing container business, United States Lines'* American Lark *was fully cellular for both 20ft and 40ft containers. With a gross tonnage of 18,876, a length of 214m and a beam of 27m, it was powered by steam turbines and capable of 23 knots. Ports of call in the UK included Tilbury, Liverpool and Greenock, and it sailed the North Atlantic calling at most ports on the Eastern Seaboard of the USA.*

The containers were lifted on and off the vessels by the recently constructed container cranes. Manufactured by Stothert & Pitt, these cranes were constructed on site between 1968 and early 1969. This view down the ship's starboard side is taken from the southeast corner of Gladstone graving dock. In the background are the construction cranes working on the site of Seaforth Dock.

Below: *This is the view from the American Lark's bridge over the length of the deck. The hatch configuration has three main hatches each at a length of forty foot: Port, Centre and Starboard. Each separate hatch had its own watertight cover that could be lifted by the container crane, and stacked on top of each other or taken ashore. The containers were moved by straddle carrier to and from the stacking area and placed under the cranes for transfer to the vessel. When loaded in the hatches the containers stacked on top of each other, while the cell guides kept them in line to prevent any movement during a voyage. The containers on the hatch top are secured to the hatch lid by locking devices in the corners of the containers and also at each vertical height upwards.*

The background of this photograph has a transit shed running from north to south. This was moved when Seaforth opened to make way for the construction of the Kellogg's Plant.

Above: *View from the top of a container crane looking at the new Seaforth Dock complex under construction, with Manchester Liners' containers stowed up to three high on the stacking area. To the left is one of the original Clark straddle carriers moving a container from the vessel to the storage area.*

Above right and right: *Two views of Atlantic Container Line vessel* Atlantic Causeway *about to enter Gladstone Lock, assisted by tugs from The Alexandra Towing Company, and the same vessel alongside the container cranes at Gladstone Container Terminal.*

CHAPTER THREE

Into the 1970s

On 6 December 1971, the Blue Star Line refrigerated general cargo ship *Tasmania Star* sailed through from Gladstone Lock into Seaforth Dock, becoming the first vessel on S2 berth designated for discharging refrigerated cargo including meat.

Early in 1972 the three new Paceco container cranes were built on the site of berths S3, 4 and 5. After commissioning the new Container Terminal in May, the two container cranes from Gladstone were moved onto barges and sailed into Seaforth for transfer to berth S5. Seaforth's opening brought closure of both the Gladstone and Hornby Container Terminals.

Although many parts were still 'under construction' the new berths soon had occupants: S7 was appropriated to West Coast Stevedoring, principally for trades with South America for Lamport & Holt Line, Houlder Brothers and Pacific Steam Navigation Co. (PSNC).

S8 and S9 were operated by MDHC as the forest products terminal, with two 'barns' or covered storage areas for sensitive cargoes such as plywood and kiln dried products.

This was probably the worst time for the Port regarding industrial relations and barely a week would go by without some sort of industrial dispute. The Grain Terminal, although finished, had yet to work a vessel due to a 'who does what' dispute between separate branches of the Transport & General Workers Union (TGWU).

Royal Seaforth opened up tremendous prospects for Liverpool and, although grain trade in particular has soared in recent years, Britain's accession to the EEC, and resultant increased trade with Europe, greatly benefited the east coast ports to the detriment of Liverpool. However, the Port maintained most of its transatlantic and Irish trade.

The industrial unrest caused considerable hardship among the remaining stevedoring companies left in the Port and it was only a matter of time before Ocean Port Services, A.E. Smith Coggins and Port of Liverpool Stevedoring came under the umbrella of MDHC Cargo Handling.

This left only three major stevedore operators: Liverpool Maritime Terminals (backed by Ocean Transport and Trading), West Coast Stevedoring Company and Harrison Line, who only handled their own vessels. Several smaller operators handled specialist cargoes and services.

The South Docks finally closed for shipping in September 1972, as the three miles of docks to the south of the city centre, with narrow quays and shallow docks, were no longer appropriate for the modern shipping trends. As a result, all major lines were allocated berths in the Northern system.

Further investment in the short sea trade was undertaken with the building of a passenger terminal at Waterloo dock for the B&I Line. Covering 17 acres of dockland and costing £2.5 million, the two-storey terminal had facilities for Customs examination, a baggage room and furnished waiting rooms. The exterior walls were covered in 13,000 square feet of clear float glass supplied by Pilkington's of St Helens.

Seaforth Dock was officially opened by Princess Anne in July 1973 and given the name Royal Seaforth Dock.

Publication of the Jones-Aldington report into dock working practices gave far greater power to the RDWs. This included working in inland container bases, sometimes several miles from the waterfront, such as Aintree Container Base – a rail and road link inland container packing station. By definition the packing and unpacking of containers was deemed to be the work of dock workers, but even a high profile court case between a haulier and the TGWU failed to reach a satisfactory solution.

The industrial strife on Merseyside was to assist the developing port of Felixstowe on the east coast. There, land reclaimed from the sea and marshes (similar to Seaforth) was being privately developed to take advantage of the container trade. It was not long before shipping companies like United States Lines moved the bigger vessels away from Liverpool, using smaller chartered tonnage to feeder between Greenock,

Scotland, Liverpool and Rotterdam. This enabled the bigger operators to reduce costs with faster transit times.

Several other operators moved away from Liverpool. Ellerman Lines, Mac Andrews and Zim moved to Ellesmere Port further up the river. Manchester Liners, however, moved in the opposite direction, transferring from Manchester to Seaforth to save the considerable time taken transiting the Ship Canal. Smaller operators also moved services to the container terminal, including Medtainer Line and a feeder service for Atlantic operator Seatrain.

The changes within the Port involved large scale voluntary severance of surplus manpower and changes in working practices, many of which were negotiated by port employers in a series of two-year pay settlements.

In June 1978 B&I Line ordered a Boeing Jetfoil with seating for 257 for service on the Liverpool to Dublin route, as this was

The changing scenes within the Port of Liverpool in the early 1970s

The final days before cutting through the North West Gladstone berth to allow passage into Seaforth.

seen as a better alternative to using hovercraft. Commencing paying passenger service in early 1980, the travelling time was 3 hours 10 minutes, making two return trips a day.

The Jetfoil *Cu Na Mara* had high operating costs and low passenger figures which, combined with her performance in bad weather, led to her being sold and the service shut down. Her arrival had been courtesy of a Johnson Line container vessel, having been loaded in Los Angeles on the starboard side of the container deck. Discharge was by MDHC floating crane *Mammoth* direct into the water of Seaforth Dock.

Below left: *Construction of the Grain Terminal storage silos.*

Below: *The final touches to the transit shed at S2 berth Seaforth. This berth would have specialist conveyor equipment for handling fresh meat and produce from South America.*

Bottom: *Construction of the Marine Towers for Seaforth Grain Terminal.*

The vessels in the ACL fleet of the 1970s

Left above: Atlantic Cognac *alongside S3 berth Royal Seaforth Dock.*

Left: Atlantic Causeway *about to enter Gladstone Lock with three tugs assisting,* Canada, Collingwood *and* Indomitable *(amidships).*

Above left: Atlantic Prelude *with Swedish Flag. Owned and operated by Wallenius Lines, this vessel was part of the service direct to Canada operating from Europe to Montreal.*

Above right: Atlantic Cinderella *(owned by Wallenius Lines) under the Swedish flag.*

Left: *T&J Harrison Line's* Astronomer *undocking at Royal Seaforth. Astronomer was the first fully cellular container vessel with self sustaining gear capable of discharging and loading containers in the non-containerised ports of the West Indies as part of the CAROL (Caribbean Overseas Lines) Consortium. It often discharged to barges while anchored off-shore. The vessel transferred to the Royal Fleet Auxiliary in 1982 and saw service in the South Atlantic after the Falklands conflict where it was re-named RFA Reliant. The conversion work was completed at the Cammell Laird shipyard at Birkenhead.*

Above: *Atlantic Container Line vessel* Atlantic Cinderella *docking at Seaforth after the terminal had opened for business. At this time only three of the five container cranes had been constructed on site; the last two cranes would be brought by barge from Gladstone Container Terminal.*

Below: *The general/reefer vessel* Rio de la Plata *from the Empresa Lineas Maritimas Argentinas SA discharging a fresh meat cargo at S2 berth Seaforth, c.1980. Built in 1971, the vessel had a gross tonnage of 10,409, a length of 153m and a beam of 21m.*

Above: *A typical general cargo vessel of the 1970s and 1980s is United Arab Shipping Companies'* Fathulkhair *pictured heading inwards in the Crosby Channel. Built in 1978, it had a gross tonnage of 15,446, a length of 175m, a beam of 23m and a service speed of 16 knots.*

One of a large fleet of general cargo ships built between 1969 and 1978, trading between Liverpool and other UK ports to Saudi Arabia, Kuwait and Iran.

Below: *A second view of a United Arab vessel,* Ibn Al Moataz, *alongside South One Gladstone.*

CHAPTER FOUR

Progress through the 1980s

At the start of the 1980s the South docks area and part of the Birkenhead docklands totalling 400 acres of land passed over to the Merseyside Development Corporation (MDC). This was achieved by Parliamentary orders set up by the Government to regenerate dockland no longer used for shipping.

Trading prospects for the first half of 1980 seemed to signify a disaster unfolding and by the end of the year they had reached an almost disastrous stage. The final figures for 1980, published in June 1981, gave a trading loss of £3.86 million. The number of man-days lost through disputes had risen dramatically from 21,235 in 1979 to 35,006 in 1980. Port employers T&J Harrison and Bulk Cargo Handling Services ceased trading with the workforces joining the MDHC. This was after other stevedoring companies, under long standing agreements with both the RDWs and the staff members of the ACTSS 5/567 branch of the TGWU, refused to accept them. This halt in trade was averted at the eleventh hour with the threat of a National dock strike.

General cargo handled within the port had dropped to 736,000 tons compared with 1,138,000 tons in 1979. Container and timber throughput was down, the latter being due to a recession in the building industry. The number of vessels using the port had dropped from 5,366 in 1979 to 4,540 in 1980.

New faces on the river include the sister tugs *Canada*, built at McTay's on Merseyside, and *Collingwood*, built at the Richard Dunstan Shipyard, Hessel. Both tugs were built for The Alexandra Towing Company and are to be based on the Mersey, these were the first omni-directional propulsion tugs employed on the river.

The new £4 million dredger *Mersey Mariner* also arrived from the Robb Caledon yard in Leith, which is part of British Shipbuilders. This is Britain's largest grab hopper dredger operating today.

As new boats arrived on the river an old 'friend' was sailing away to the breakers yard. Isle of Man Steam Packet steamer *Mona's Isle* was towed from her berth at Birkenhead to a breakers yard in the Netherlands. Having given twenty-nine years of service on the Irish Sea route she ended her tour of duty after the summer season of 1980.

By the winter of 1980 B&I Line had suspended the Jetfoil service between Liverpool and Dublin without definite plans to resume it in the spring. Despite making 475 Irish sea crossings, carrying over 75,000 passengers and giving a reliability performance of 94 per cent, the future was uncertain.

The summer of 1981 will be long remembered by employees of the Port past and present as the worst time in Liverpool's history since the financial crash of 1971. Several blows culminated in the loss of £9 million worth of trade throughout the port.

The major shipping lines of Manchester Liners and Johnson Scan Star moved to Felixstowe on the east coast, the Tate & Lyle sugar business closed, Central Electricity Generating Board (CEGB) closed at Birkenhead and Burmah Oil pulled out of the Tranmere Oil Terminal and the Stanlow refinery. Industrial disputes both inside and outside the dock estate (road haulage contractors blocked the dock gates at Seaforth in one dispute) caused loss of income of nearly £1 million. The future

Tug Canada *pictured awaiting her next duty inbound.*

container terminal would lose over £5 million with the loss of Manchester Liners & Johnson Scan Star.

Possibly the biggest change to the registered dock workforce, since decasualisation, came in September 1981. The labour force of RDWs were now all based at one labour control point at Gladstone Dock, situated behind the Latex tanks to the rear of South 1. This gave greater control of resources to the employer. Previously, the MDHC had groups of workers in areas such as West Langton, Seaforth, Huskisson and the coastwise control at Princes half-tide dock. Concentration of trades within the general cargo areas was in the main within Gladstone Dock with berths at North 1 Alexandra and West Langton not too far away. The labour force for the Seaforth complex, apart from specialist operators at the grain terminal, came from this source. Men employed in specific areas would be pre-allocated by rota

for a week's employment thus ending time lost travelling from berth to berth. This became the way of working for the majority, with only ship gangs retaining the 'old fashioned status' of working at a hatch until it is either fully discharged or fully loaded. This gave the employer greater flexibility over manning, time keeping and cost savings.

With the changing fortunes within the Port, two-year pay deals for all divisions of MDHC were just one of the major negotiating powers that combined with both the workforces and the company management. This method of business was to prove the way forward to achieve profitability later in the 1980s.

Several changes occurred at the container terminal. One of the two transit sheds used for packing and unpacking containers was mothballed due in the main to the increasing number of house-to-house containers per vessel. This was under 40 per cent

Manchester Concorde *is pictured passing through* Gladstone Dock *en route to the lock. The familiar red-hulled vessels maintained the service until the early 1980s when the service was taken over by Orient Overseas Container* Line (OOCL) *and relocated to Felixstowe on the east coast, this class of vessel being replaced by a larger one.*

in the 1960s, but the figure was reaching the high eighties by the end of 1981. Only the under-developed countries of West Africa, some Central American countries and the west coast of South America retained pier to pier status.

The older maintenance depot at Dacre Street was closed in favour of moving close to the Labour Control base at North Hornby. A further blow to the Port's fortunes followed when P&O announced the closure of the service between Northern Ireland and Princes dock, which had been carried out by the two sister vessels *Ulster Prince* and *Ulster Queen*. Despite pleas to the Government for help, the 150-year-old service finally closed on 12 October 1981. The two vessels remained for several months in Princes Dock before being sold.

Car exports for the Irish market from Ford's factory at Halewood on Merseyside continued to be shipped from Royal Seaforth's S6 berth, while large quantities of Fiat cars arrived from Italy in the same method of drive on, drive off. This traffic had now been established for three years.

On the same July day in 1981 that B&I Lines' new building arrived in the river, an old servant to the port, ACL's *Atlantic Conveyor*, moved from Seaforth's S3 berth to a lay-up berth at North West Canada via the river. The future was uncertain for this 1969-built vessel.

After a lengthy stay alongside sister vessel *Atlantic Causeway*, she was requisitioned by the Ministry of Defence to form part of the taskforce to sail for the Falkland Islands in the spring of 1982. Converted with the use of containers on the wing positions, this taskforce included liquid tank containers carrying both fresh water and fuel for the cargo of helicopters and vertical-take-off Sea Harriers. The container deck provided an excellent landing base with a little help from the MOD at Devonport dockyard.

Mediterranean Express, *shown here in Seaforth Dock, was the main vessel used for moving cars between Liverpool and Ireland. The dual purpose vessel could also be used for carrying livestock.*

Above: Conveyor *at Ascension Island, courtesy of Chief Petty Officer*
Bob Gellett.

Right: *MOD picture of a Harrier landing on* Conveyor's *forward deck.*

Final pictures of the Atlantic Conveyor, *Falkland Islands, May 1982. These graphic pictures of the fire-ravaged* Atlantic Conveyor *were taken shortly before the vessel sank off the Falkland Islands. Twelve men, including the Master Ian North, died after an Argentine Exocet missile hit the ship.*

The pictures, taken from the Hull tug Irishman, *shocked ACL staff ashore and afloat who knew the* Atlantic Conveyor *well. Although the superstructure is badly ravaged, containers are still firmly fastened to the deck.*

The Irishman, *owned by United Towing Limited (a member of the North British Maritime Group), managed to bring the* Atlantic Conveyor *under tow when fog descended. The towline parted and the blip on the tug's radar disappeared indicating that* Atlantic Conveyor *had sunk. This was one of the last pictures of the ship before she sank. Two members of the* Irishman's *crew twice boarded the still-burning* Atlantic Conveyor *to put towlines on board; both men were awarded the British Empire Medal (BEM).*

Several other vessels with Liverpool connections were involved in the Falklands conflict. ACL's Atlantic Causeway *(sister ship to the* Conveyor*) and Harrison Line's* Astronomer *both sailed south carrying a variety of men and equipment. (Photographs courtesy Cunard/ACL)*

Below: *Order of Service at Liverpool Cathedral, July 1982.*

LIVERPOOL CATHEDRAL

A REMEMBRANCE OF THOSE
WHO DIED
IN THE
'ATLANTIC CONVEYOR'
AND FOR ALL OTHERS
INVOLVED IN THE SOUTH ATLANTIC CONFLICT

Thursday, July 1st 1982 at 12 noon

Above: *The taskforce also requisitioned Ocean Transport & Trading's* Sapele, *pictured here.*

Below: *Belfast Car Ferries started a one-vessel daily sailing between Langton Dock and Belfast in June 1982 (some eight months after P&O Lines' withdrawal). Sailing seven days a week at 11a.m. each morning, the vessel* St Colum I *(built in 1973, 5,285grt) pictured swinging in Gladstone Dock prior to entering the lock, berthed here alongside the old Langton Branch Dock, the transit shed being used for car marshalling prior to boarding. This vessel also carried freight and trade cars.*

Royal Seaforth continued to improve reliability and productivity and several new breeds of straddle carrier were purchased. They were bigger, faster and capable of stacking 40ft containers three high. The first generation could only park 40ft containers two high. Several major companies also came and went. ACT, whose companies included Cunard, Blue Star Line, Port Line and Harrison Line, moved to Tilbury on London's river Thames. In the early 1980s the quaysides would remain empty for days between vessel calls. Only the ACL (who had closed their Southampton operation in favour of Liverpool), CONPAC and the CAROL Consortium of Harrison's, KNSM, CGM and Hapag-Lloyd remained as 'big' ship operators. Smaller operators came to Liverpool, including Celtic Freight with chartered tonnage who operated a weekly service to Portugal. The line's principals were Cardiff-based Charles M. Willie & Co. MedAfrica started a service between Liverpool and West Africa that only lasted a few months. Furness Withy operated a roll-on, roll-off container service (Streamline) on a monthly basis with two vessels sailing between Europe and Central America. Canada Maritime was formed by CMB Belgium and Canadian Pacific and operated container/timber/roll-on, roll-off services with regular shipments of over 4,000 tons of block stowed Canadian timber.

Another consortium, Eurosal, operated from Liverpool with five 1,915teu (twenty foot equivalent unit) capacity vessels sailing with a twenty-four day frequency. The vessels catered for both the container and conventional trade of copper, and capacity in excess of 9,000 tons could be stowed underneath the normal container stowage. Eurosal consortium members included PSNC, Transnave of Equador (TNE), Compania Sud Americana de Vapores SA (CSAV), Hapag-Lloyd and Sweden's Johnson Line. Each of the sister vessels is equipped with its own rail-mounted container gantry capable of lifting 30.5 tons. Sensitive cargoes such as bananas can be ripened during the voyage in temperature-controlled containers. Large quantities of coffee were carried in ventilated containers.

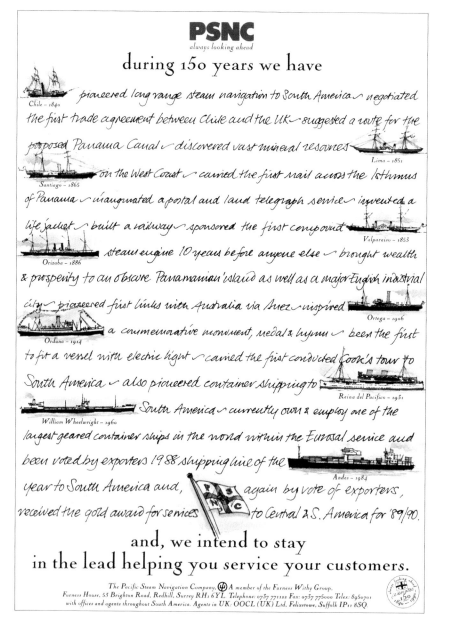

A PSNC full-page advertisement from the late 1980s.

In the spring of 1984 the Port witnessed the first of the new third-generation container roll-on, roll-off ships from Atlantic Container Line (ACL). *Atlantic Companion* arrived in March followed by two more vessels: *Compass* and *Concert*. The last two of the ACL fleet, *Cartier* and Cunard's *Conveyor* arrived in early 1985.

It was during this period that the workforce negotiated with the MDHC an agreement to work whenever an ACL vessel docked over the weekend. Weekday working was still covered by three-shift working. The new weekend work plan had flexible starting times to meet the arrival of the vessel. With the size of these vessels, arrival in the river would be approximately two hours before high water with the need to sail before high water on the next tide. Allowing time to lock in and out of Gladstone Lock and for passage to and from the S3 berth, this would give eleven hours working time for containers, car loadings and roll-on, roll-off operations.

During 1984 and early 1985 industrial strife in the port of Southampton worked in Liverpool's favour. With the southern container terminal closed, the larger vessels of the SAECS consortium trading between South Africa and Europe relocated to Liverpool, albeit on a temporary basis. Overseas Containers (OCL), Nedlloyd and Safmarine ships of 55,000 tons gross visited Seaforth, all being handled efficiently and to schedule with a background of vastly improved industrial relations.

After making a small profit in 1983, Mersey Docks made a profit of £800,000 on a turnover of some £50 million in 1984. Tonnages were slightly in excess of nine million, but that year was to be the turning point in the port's fortunes.

As the fortunes of Seaforth grew, the general cargo traffic was steadily going in the opposite direction. Countries such as Saudi Arabia and those in regions such as West Africa and South America were moving towards containerisation. Many of the vessels working in the general cargo areas of the Port handled containers as well as large volumes of general cargo. A good example of this traffic could be seen in the Huskisson/Canada Dock area, where vessels of the UKWAL group, including

Ocean (Elder Dempster), Guinea Gulf Line, Nigerian National Line and Palm Line berthed. Container handling would be done at North 3 Canada with the general cargo discharged and loaded at North 1 Huskisson Dock.

Several other operators (such as Unithai) traded between Gladstone Dock and Malaysia, Singapore and Thailand in conjunction with the Malaysian International Shipping Company (MISC). The service used several 'old friends' of the Liverpool waterfront.

The tonnage supplied was the previously-owned 'Strath' boats from P&O.

New Name	Date Built	P&O Name	Date Changed	Break up Date
Anchan	1967	*Strathardle*	1979	Aug. 1986
Benjamas	1967	*Strathbora*	1979	Oct. 1986
Jumpa	1970	*Strathmay*★	1982	Jan. 1988
Kannikar	1971	*Strathmeigle*★★	1975	Sep. 1987
Intanin	1971	*Strathmore*★★★	1975	Aug. 1986

★ Built as *Manora*
★★ Built as *Merkara*
★★★ Built as *Morvada*

The United Arab Shipping Company also used Gladstone Dock, trading with Saudi Arabia, Kuwait, United Arab Emirates, Iran and Iraq. Previously these vessels had used the West Langton and West Brocklebank berths when higher volumes were exported from Liverpool.

The general cargo trade with South and Central America was more import than export. Similar to most companies, the PSNC joined a consortium for container traffic and used the older general cargo vessels from the 1960s and early 1970s for a mix of general cargo and containers. This type of trading would mirror several other shipping companies such as Harrison Line, Booth Line and Lamport & Holt Line.

A selection of pictures of the five 'Strath' boats, showing in detail the deck cranes and the heavy lift Stülcken derrick between the hatches on the fore deck.

Elsewhere in the Port at North East Hornby, roll-on, roll-off services sailed nightly to the Isle of Man. Several containers were also packed and unpacked daily on site by the local workforce employed by Ireman Stevedoring Co. on behalf of the Isle of Man Steam Packet Co.

The MD&HC's grain terminal had direct feeds by conveyor to three major mills: Kellogg's, who opened Seaforth mill in 1973, Allied Mills and Cargill, who took over the soya bean plant from the Continental Grain Co. of New York. Smaller grain operators use Birkenhead's East Float and Liverpool grain storage facility at Alexandra Dock. Although no longer accessible to waterborne traffic, Brunswick Dock silos were still used for storage. The Timber Terminal attracted more than 100 vessel calls in 1986 for such operators as Sanko Line and Gearbulk as well as regular calls from Russian shipping interests.

Passenger traffic on a large scale had disappeared with the last of the Cunard liners in the late 1960s. Canadian Pacific and Elder Dempster had all left the port, leaving only the short sea crossings to the Isle of Man and Ireland for passengers.

B&I Lines' lift-on, lift-off container service at Waterloo Dock closed in favour of roll-on, roll-off traffic in conjunction with Pandoro (P&O). B&I Line retained the passenger/freight service's daily sailings from the award-winning Trafalgar Dock terminal. B&I had moved to this terminal from Carriers Dock. Two 'new' vessels were operating the service. The *Leinster* (built 1981, 6,900grt) arrived in July 1981 and the *Connacht* (built 1979, 6,800grt) used Waterloo river entrance until 1983, when economies within the MDHC made it no longer viable to keep the river entrance open. With very little other traffic using the entrance, the costs of dredging and twenty-four hour manpower coverage made the closure essential for the future of the port. The *Connacht* made the last voyage on 18 October 1983, with *Leinster* being the first to arrive at Brocklebank, docking stern first to a newly purpose-built ramp at the east end close to the Dock Road.

B&I Line's berth at Brocklebank Branch Dock was the former home to Elder Dempster's general cargo in the 1960s. The berth was adapted for passengers and roll-on, roll-off traffic. The site of the former Langton graving docks was infilled for vehicle marshalling. The former B&I container crane at Waterloo dock was moved up to Seaforth's S6 berth for future short sea container workings.

This was virtually the end of 'the coast area' as it was known, with only limited traffic using the smaller docks to the south of Sandon Dock. One of these smaller areas was a focal point for imports of bulk rum for vessels docking at South Nelson Dock, with cargo being discharged via pipeline to MDHC's bonded Stanley Warehouse. The majority of other docks at this time in this area now had either limited use or had fallen into disrepair.

Sadly, the B&I link of 152 years ended on 6 January 1988 with *Connacht* making the last sailing from Dublin. It should be stated that B&I did have serious financial problems throughout the 1960s, 1970s and 1980s before the Irish Government-owned company was finally sold to Irish Continental Line in 1992.

A replacement service commenced from the same berth with Sealink's roll-on, roll-off *Earl William* on 25 April 1988, sailing at 10.30p.m. nightly and returning during the following daytime to arrive at 6.30p.m., seven days a week. With a capacity of 500 passengers and 120 cars, the vessel docked at Dun Laoghaire as the Eire port of call.

The year 1986 was one of tremendous significance, as not a single day was lost in the Port by any form of work stoppage. This was a far cry from the 1970s and helped Liverpool's image considerably.

The year 1987 was a landmark for The Alexandra Towing Company, one of the major tug operators on the Mersey, as it celebrated 100 years of towage. Several companies had been bought by ATCL, namely North West Tugs in 1951 and J.H. Lamey in 1968. Alexandra Towing was the major container ship handler in the Port, and often up to three boats would dock one of the ACL vessels or a large bulk carrier at the grain terminal.

Liverpool had a fleet of eleven boats, including the *Brocklebank* working at Barrow. Of the remaining ten, three had been built for the developing container trade. With Voith Schneider propulsion, the tugs' manoeuvrability ensured a safe docking.

(Photograph courtesy of Hal Mullin, Wirral)

Selection of postcards celebrating The
Alexandra Towing Company's centenary

Rea Towing Co., owned by the Ocean Group, was also a major tug operator, with a variety of tugs capable of handling smaller barge traffic to berthing the larger oil tankers visiting Tranmere Oil Terminal on the Birkenhead side of the Mersey.

In 1987 discussions between ACL and Hapag-Lloyd resulted in slot chartering on both companies' vessels from European ports to the USA and Canada. The five third-generation G3 vessels were lengthened by 42m in shipyards in the Far East and Greenock, Scotland. Hapag-Lloyd would slot charter on ACL's Liverpool sailing with reciprocal agreements on Hapag sailings from other ports, improving transit times and reducing road haulage costs. As a result, Hapag ceased direct calls at Greenock in favour of Liverpool.

To improve relations within the companies, two of the G3 fleet had the Hapag name *Express* added after the original ACL name i.e. *Atlantic Companion* became *Companion Express*, and two of the Hapag fleet acquired the name *Atlantic* instead of Express i.e. *Koln Express* became *Koln Atlantic*.

By the end of the 1980s the MDHC had turned in a profit each year since 1983. Developments during the 1980s included the re-laying of railway tracks through to a purpose-built Freightliner terminal at Seaforth, the first containers to arrive by rail since Gladstone in 1967. The point of access was still across the Dock Road at the site of Alexandra Goods Station (long since closed

The two ACL vessels in dock with four ATCL Tugs.

for railway business). However, it did a have a new lease of life in the 1970s when containers of mail for Royal Mail were handled prior to shipment on board the container services from the Port.

After crossing on to MDHC land, the rail containers passed adjacent to the road, normally crossing Strand Road dock gate at the busiest time of the day. They then stayed inside the dock estate on the perimeter of Gladstone Dock and finally passed between Kellogg's mill and the grain terminal before entering the double-tracked Freightliner terminal. Transfer to rail wagons from tractor and vice versa was by a Morris overhead gantry crane capable of spanning both tracks and a specific lane for container trailer haulage. This method of distribution was used extensively for the SAECS services during late 1984 and early 1985 for delivery to the respective container bases throughout the country.

Although the MDHC was profitable in this period, many people had left the industry; both RDWs and clerical staff from the dock estate and within the Port of Liverpool Building. The number of workers required in all sections of the Port was reduced as shipping offices closed and ship repair and ship supply facilities scaled down business to meet present day demands. Investment was dependant on profitability for the future of the Port.

The period of 1984-85 was to be a major turning point in the Seaforth Container terminal's fortunes. The workforce now had a proven record of reliability to seek new business from customers old and new, and this relatively dispute-free period led to stability within other areas of the port. This was especially true of general cargo, grain, timber and the short sea ferry operators.

One of the newer trades to arrive in the Port of Liverpool was scrap metal. Launched in 1982, Seahorn Marine began operating from the north side of No.1 Canada Dock, loading scrap metal for a variety of destinations within Europe and as far afield as India. This trade was to grow throughout the 1980s and 1990s, piling the once-traditional quaysides from Seaforth to Canada Dock with mountains of scrap metal.

The MDHC introduced the new Mersey Mammoth to the river in November 1986 as part of a £17 million capital cost for fleet replacement. Mersey Mammoth cost £4.5 million, having been built by Figee of Haarlem and shipyard Ravestein of Deest, Holland. The self-propelled crane is capable of heavy lift, carrying up to 250 tons by its main hoist, and is equipped with a 50-ton auxiliary hoist that also has the ability to work by grab, lifting bulk cargoes at a capacity of 400 tons per hour. With a crew of eight including the master, she sails at a speed of 7 knots and has a deck load of 640 tons.

The former site of south Brocklebank/Carriers Dock/Brocklebank Graving Dock was infilled to make the site ready for Bibby Edible Oils Ltd when they completed the move from central Liverpool. This £35 million complex was planned to take the company into the twenty-first century.

By the end of 1988, two new trades had moved to Royal Seaforth's container terminal. Previous customer Ocean Transport & Trading's decision to switch from 'combi' operations (containers and general cargo) to a pure container operation caused their move. The second trade was new business to Liverpool. Balt-Canada Line, operated by Morline on behalf of the Anglo Soviet Shipping Co., transferred operations from Felixstowe. A further boost to the terminal was the forthcoming move from Garston, further down the river, to Seaforth's S6 berth for Coastal Containers' daily services to Belfast.

The south docks had undergone a massive change, since closure in 1972, through Merseyside Development Corporation. Docks previously silted up had been drained and cleaned, and the Merseyside Maritime Museum took a prime site close to the city centre on the edge of Canning Dock, with waterborne exhibits alongside. The Albert Dock complex was renovated as both a shopping complex and a television studio. Several acres were cleared south of the Albert Dock area for future developments. At Wapping, the former dock warehouses adjacent to the main road were converted into flats and a similar plan was proposed for the warehouses at Waterloo Dock.

The Bibby Complex looking towards Liverpool City Centre.

South Brocklebank Dock, Bibby Complex at night.

Liverpool Docks FOUR DECADES OF CHANGE

The transit sheds around Brunswick, Toxteth and Harrington Docks were converted into small business units with some of the bigger, former dock sheds accommodating major customers. The water areas were infilled to form large vehicle access areas.

In the summer of 1985 Liverpool had a rather interesting visitor. Arriving by sea into Gladstone Lock to tie up alongside Seaforth's east quayside was *Virgin Atlantic Challenger*. Soon to be lifted from the water to a specialist ACL trailer, this was the craft destined to make an attempt on the fastest crossing between America and Europe. After shipment on board ACL's *Atlantic Compass*, the craft was bound for New York after discharging at Halifax, Nova Scotia.

Several of the sailing crew stayed until the ship was safely on board, overseeing the lifting and securing. The prize at stake was the Hales Trophy. Known as the Blue Riband of the Atlantic, this was presented by Harold K. Hales, MP for Hanley, Stoke-on-Trent, on 22 August 1935 for international competition to be held by the ship making the fastest crossing between Europe and America.

The previous holder was SS *United States*, which took the award in 1952 from the *Queen Mary* when she averaged 35.59 knots. As the *Virgin Atlantic Challenger* was under way in the North Atlantic, she developed a fuel oil fault requiring emergency refuelling. An RAF Nimrod spotter plane shadowing the craft made contact with the ACL vessel *Atlantic Service* (former name *Atlantic Span*) and after radio contact arranged a rendezvous to supply the fuel by partially lowering the stern ramp in mid-Atlantic to transfer several drums of lube oil.

Another Liverpool company assisted with the record attempt. Alexandra Towing provided a deep sea tug, *Indomitable*, to refuel on the crossing. She fought her way 600 miles out into the North Atlantic through a full-blooded gale, and there kept station for two and a half days, rolling in a lumpy sea, as she awaited the 60ft catamaran. The *Indomitable* did her work

Looking through the gable arch of Salthouse Dock towards the city centre.

quickly and efficiently to keep the attempt alive but, within striking distance of completion, disaster struck the Virgin craft and the record attempt failed some two hours from the finishing line. All on board were rescued before the craft finally broke up and sank.

The following year *Virgin Atlantic Challenger II* took up the challenge of another attempt. Following the same route pattern, this craft sailed on board ACL's *Atlantic Cartier*, this time crossing the finishing line within the time allowed.

After some eight years of major changes and modernisation, including numerous redundancies, the Port braced itself for what was to come in the summer of 1989. The Conservative Government, under the leadership of Margaret Thatcher, decided to abolish the National Dock Labour Board scheme guaranteeing 'jobs for life' for registered dockworkers. What followed was not unexpected: a national dock strike. Backed by Government funding, most of the 'scheme' ports as they were known were to see vast numbers of RDWs leave the industry with a golden handshake of £35,000.

50

Virgin Atlantic Challenger I *and* II.

One of the famous shipping lines with Liverpool connections was Blue Star Line, once with a vast fleet of general cargo and reefer vessels. The fleet changed dramatically between the mid-1980s and the latter stages of the 1990s. Previously, all the BSL fleet would be United Kingdom-registered and fly the 'red ensign' or 'red duster' as it was affectionately known. Pictured at Royal Seaforth's S2 berth discharging refrigerated and general cargo in 1984 is Timaru Star. In the background on S3 berth is ACL's Atlantic Crown.

After a six-week dispute, the national strike ended with settlement in all ports except Liverpool. The Liverpool men returned a week later after seeking guarantees of future employment and union recognition. The much-reduced Liverpool workforce returned to work by marching in solidarity to the dock gates, several hundred men having 'taken the money' during the national strike.

While the dispute continued, the MDHC made significant plans for the future. The labour control at Hornby Dock was closed in favour of localised work forces permanently employed in specific areas. In Liverpool, this was to pave the way for new contracts of employment for men returning to work, with new manning scales and greater working flexibility.

The general cargo area at North 2 Canada Dock came under the name of Liverpool Cargo Handling, which took over the general cargo operations. Dedicated workforces were located at the container and timber terminals with a coastwise team handling the Irish ferry vessels at Brocklebank Dock. Union recognition remained under the umbrella of the TGWU. However, the days of the powerful 'shop steward' were overtaken by worker committees with a lot less power.

Other UK ports had completely overhauled workforces, and contract labour (non-union, casual labour) returned in many ports. This had been one of the main things the port workforces had stood against for many years.

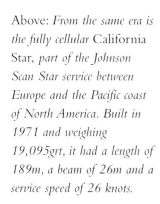

Above: *From the same era is the fully cellular* California Star, *part of the Johnson Scan Star service between Europe and the Pacific coast of North America. Built in 1971 and weighing 19,095grt, it had a length of 189m, a beam of 26m and a service speed of 26 knots.*

Below: *Another JSS consortium member was the Danish Company the East Asiatic Co. They supplied two vessels,* Falstria, *and, pictured here,* Meonia.

Blue Star Line was one of the partners in Associated Container Transportation (ACT), a consortium of shipping companies trading between Europe, Australia and New Zealand. Other partners included Port Line (Cunard) BSL and Australian National Line (ANL). One of the ACT fleet, ACT 4, is pictured heading out from Gladstone Lock into the river. Built in 1971, it weighed 24,907grt, had a length of 217m, a beam of 29m and a service speed of 22 knots.

Above: *Latterly the Blue Star fleet consisted of older vessels registered in a variety of offshore countries and chartered tonnage. An example of Blue Star Line chartered tonnage, Saxon Star is shown here under the German flag. Built in 1979, it weighed 10,153grt, had a length of 168m, a beam of 23m and a service speed of 21 knots. This type of vessel, although fully cellular, had reefer facilities within the hatches under deck to chill, freeze or ripen temperature-controlled cargo during voyages.*

Below: *The consortium trading between Europe and Pacific ports of the United States was known as 'Conpac'. Its members included CGM of France, Hapag-Lloyd of Germany and KNSM and Incotrans of Holland. The CGM member vessel pictured here is Lafayette, inbound in the Crosby Channel. Built in 1978 and weighing 27,305grt, it had a length of 204m, a beam of 31m and a service speed of 22 knots.*

Above: *Various Russian trades have used the Port of Liverpool for many years, ranging from small Baltic timber vessels through to the container revolution. Pictured on the Timber Terminal is the combi-vessel* Sverdlovsk *with a mixed cargo of containers and general cargo.*

Below: *Part of the service to East Africa from Europe,* Polesk *is pictured alongside S4 berth of the container terminal.*

Transnave combi vessel Isla Baltra *is pictured at South 2 Gladstone Dock. Trading between Europe and the west coast of South America, this service transferred to a fully cellular container service – Eurosal – in the mid 1980s.*

Above: *South 1 Gladstone Dock in March 1984. Once the home to Blue Funnel general cargo vessels, this area of the Port was now in use for loading general cargo in a variety of trades. On the east berth is a United Arab Ibn-class loading for the Arabian Gulf and Kuwait, while on the west berth is a former P&O general cargo vessel, now in the colours of Unithai and named* Kannikar.

Below: *The last of the Lamport & Holt Line fleet,* Romney *is berthed at South West 2 Gladstone Dock. Built for Bank Line as the* Ruddbank *in 1979, she joined the Lamport Fleet in 1983. This vessel, along with several other Liverpool regulars, discharged in Liverpool prior to loading in Bristol with general cargo for the Falkland Islands, including materials for the rebuilding of the airport after the 1982 conflict. With a gross tonnage of 12,214, she had a length of 162m, a beam of 23m and a service speed of 16 knots.*

Rea Towing Ltd, one of the main tug operators in the Port of Liverpool, had a variety of boats for the changing trends. Pictured in the early 1980s is the Foylegarth *heading inwards in Gladstone Lock. Also visible are general cargo vessels working either side of the middle group of transit sheds.*

Liverpool has various trades importing timber, including the Far East and Canada. Pictured discharging a timber cargo in the early 1980s is C.P. Ships' *bulk carrier* **Fort Kamloops,** *built in 1976, weighing 17,280grt, with a length of 173m, a beam of 25m and a service speed of 15 knots.*

Above: *Two views of Palm Line vessels in Huskisson Dock in the early 1980s. The older vessel is* Africa Palm *berthed at the west end of No.1 Branch Dock. Built in 1971 and weighing 10,008grt, she had a length of 153m, a beam of 20m and a service speed of 18 knots.*

Below: *The second vessel is* Lagos Palm *berthed in No.3 Branch Dock. Built in 1981 and weighing 15,575grt, she had a length of 177m, a beam of 25m and a service speed of 18 knots.*

These pictures give a good comparison of the changing styles of shipbuilding. The older vessel has standard lifting derricks at hatches one and four with a heavy lift Stülc ken derrick between hatches two and three, while the later build has lifting capacity for most container type loads and weights at all hatches. Although the later ship has a tween deck, this can be left open for container stacking from the lower hold to the highest point under deck.

Above: *The West Africa trade was made up of famous names including Elder Dempster, Guinea Gulf Line, Palm Line and Ocean. All traded from Liverpool to the West African coast. The Nigerian National Line joined the trading group, originally called Africa Container Express (ACE), and was later known as UKWAL when Ocean and NNL were the main operators. The Nigerian National Shipping Line vessel pictured is* River Oji *at Huskisson Dock.*

Below: *Atlantic Container Line third generation vessel* Atlantic Cartier *is pictured arriving on her maiden voyage under the French flag. This was CGM's contribution to the five vessel fleet in 1985. Assisting her towards Gladstone Lock are* Canada, Collingwood *and* Bramley Moore, *three tugs from The Alexandra Towing Company fleet. To the extreme right is the framework of the West Alexandra Dock shed in the process of being demolished.*

CHAPTER FIVE

Mersey Miscellany

Two views of the launch of a Type 22 Frigate for the Royal Navy. F82 HMS Campbeltown, launched 7 October 1987, is pictured heading down the slipway and in the river being safely collected by tugs from The Alexandra Towing Company. Waterloo is the lead boat on the bow rope, with Collingwood on the stern. Also visible to the right are the refurbished south docks sheds and warehouses.

Above: *Hapag-Lloyd Container Vessel* Caribia Express *outward bound at the mouth of the river Mersey passing channel buoy C20 in 1984. Built in 1976 and weighing 27,971grt, she had a length of 204m, a beam of 31m and a service speed of 21 knots.*

Below: *A second picture alongside S5 Royal Seaforth shows* Caribia Express, *one of a fleet of vessels operated by the CAROL consortium to and from the West Indies, loading containers.*

The CAROL consortium was typical of container trades after the 1970s. Several shipping lines would combine space on each other's vessels making numerous savings and giving a regular timetable for the lines' customers. This consortium had a fleet of ships built to the same design at the same Polish shipyard but for each separate owner to operate.

The design included a self-sustaining facility to discharge and load containers from the ship's own travelling container crane on board. Positioned at the bay forward of the bridge, this crane can travel the length of the vessel on rails when the ship is in port or at an anchorage to discharge to a barge. This facility gave advantages to container operators who used ports in Central America and the West Indies that did not have container cranes or deep water berthing facilities.

The ships in the consortium carried the colours of Hapag-Lloyd (Germany), CGM (France) and KNSM (the Netherlands), which was later taken over by Nedlloyd Lines and Harrison Line (United Kingdom).

Above: *Booth Steamship Company general cargo/container vessel* Benedict, *registered in Liverpool, pictured alongside S4 berth Royal Seaforth Container Terminal in 1985. Built in 1979 along with sister vessel* Boniface, *these were the last two directly-owned vessels of the Booth Line, part of the Blue Star Group. When they were sold in the late 1980s they were replaced by chartered tonnage for several years before the trading name of Booth Line, once famous in Liverpool, disappeared altogether. Weighing 3,636grt, the vessel had a length of 116m, a beam of 17m and a service speed of 15 knots.*

Below: *One of the most famous names in the Port of Liverpool was Blue Funnel Line, latterly known as Ocean Transport & Trading Co. This line, formed in 1865 by Alfred Holt as the Ocean Steamship Co., traded all over the world with its base in India Building, Water Street, Liverpool. The last vessel to carry an Ocean name was* Menelaus, *the fifth with that name. Her last voyage for Ocean was on 30 March 1989 and she was the last of the fleet, it having been sold to Hong Kong Chinese. She is pictured here heading out through the Crosby Channel, having discharged her last cargo of containers from West Africa the previous day at the container terminal.*

Built by Mitsubishi Heavy Industries, Nagasaki, in 1977 as one of a fleet of six similar vessels from that period, Menelaus *had a gross tonnage of 16,031, a length of 165m, a beam of 26m and a service speed of 18 knots. Sister vessels had the traditional Blue Funnel names of* Memnon, Maron, Melampus, Menetheus *and* Myrmidon.

Above: *During the latter part of 1984 and the early part of 1985 the Port of Liverpool became the temporary home for the SAECS Consortium when the Port of Southampton closed during an industrial dispute. There was a ten day service northbound discharging containers from South Africa including many with fresh produce. After several other European port calls to load for the same destination, the ships would return to South Africa again. Consortium members included Safmarine (South Africa), Overseas Containers Limited (UK), DAL (Germany), CMB (Belgium) and Nedlloyd (the Netherlands). Pictured alongside S5 berth Royal Seaforth Container Terminal is S.A. Helderberg. Built in 1977 and weighing 53,023grt, she had a length of 258m, a beam of 32m, a speed of 21 knots and was powered by twin-screw diesel engines.*

Below: *Heading towards Gladstone Lock from Seaforth is sister vessel S.A. Winterberg. At that time this size of vessel was the largest to enter Seaforth Dock and the Gladstone river entrance.*

CHAPTER SIX

Modern Port Images of Royal Seaforth Docks

A German container vessel chartered by Andrew Weir Shipping, City of Dublin is loading containers at night at S4 berth, Royal Seaforth Container Terminal. The terminal is open for vessels 24 hours each day, seven days each week and only closes for Christmas Day, Boxing Day and New Year's Day.

Laser Lines' (formerly Johnson Lines') Bo Johnson *from the Grain Terminal, with the tug* Herkules *pushing amidships towards the quayside.* Herkules *was later to be renamed* Gladstone *in keeping with the Alexandra Towing Co. tradition.*

Right: *A second picture of* Bo Johnson, *this time entering Royal Seaforth Dock assisted by two tugs in the colours of The Alexandra Towing Co.* Canada *is on the bow rope and* Bramley Moore *is on the stern.*

In the background, having departed earlier, is a Russian combi-vessel that is capable of handling containers and roll-on, roll-off traffic via the quarter ramp visible at the stern.

Below: *German chartered vessel* Gracechurch Crown *pictured heading towards Gladstone Lock.* Gracechurch Crown *was able to access the Liverpool lock system at any time regardless of tide, having previously operated from Garston where tidal access was restricted.*

Below right: *Departing from Gladstone Lock is Dutch flagged coaster* Commodore *chartered by Railfreight Distribution for container traffic between Liverpool and Ireland.*

Close up of the tug Collingwood *assisting Russian container vessel* Nikolay
Golovanov *towards her berth at Royal Seaforth.*

Departing from Royal Seaforth Dock and heading towards Gladstone Lock is the Pacific Steam Navigation Co. (PSNC) vessel Andes. Built in 1984 and having a gross tonnage of 32,152, she had a length of 203m, a beam of 32m and a service speed of 15 knots.

Andes was sailing between Europe and the west coast of South America as part of the Eurosal group of companies that included Hapag-Lloyd of Germany, Transnave of Equador, Nedlloyd of Holland and Compania Sud Americana de Vapores SA (CSAV) of Chile. The sister vessels would operate on the service and each was built to a similar design but in the colours of their respective owners. Each vessel had a moveable container crane fixed on the deck and was capable of discharging and loading containers in ports that did not have specialist container lifting cranes (container crane pictured amidships).

The containers would be slot chartered by the consortium to give equal trading shares on all vessels. This increased the frequency of sailings, giving a major benefit to shippers.

Above: *Waiting in Gladstone Lock is Hapag-Lloyd's Caribia Express. Owned by Hapag-Lloyd, it operated as part of the CAROL consortium to Central American and West Indian ports. Built in 1976 in Poland, it weighed 27,971grt, had a length of 204m, a beam of 31m and a service speed of 21 knots.*

Pictured in the late 1980s, this is also a good view of the site to the east of Gladstone Lock. Alongside the Gladstone-Hornby passage, the dock master's house is visible on the left. This was used as living accommodation for MDHB staff working on the lock. Also visible are the 'Boat House' offices, the North Hornby Transit Shed and the quayside cranes. In the background is a Nigerian National Line vessel in Alexandra Dock.

Below: Nedlloyd Hollandia, *another member of the CAROL consortium and built to the same specifications, was originally built for KNSM as* Hollandia. *She is pictured alongside the quay at Royal Seaforth Container Terminal in 1984. On S6 berth is a submarine and in the background an Isle of Man Steam Packet passenger vessel navigates the Crosby Channel at low water heading for Princes Landing Stage.*

The sole Liverpool-based member of the consortium is T&J Harrison Ltd. Known as Harrison Line, they supplied three vessels between 1976 and the 1990s. Maintaining Harrison Line traditional names, they are called Astronomer, Adviser *and* Author. *All were built to similar specifications.*

Harrison Line's Adviser *is about to depart from Seaforth for Gladstone Lock on a calm day with only one tug taking the bow rope. The Harrison funnel was affectionately known as 'two fat and one of lean' dateing back to when Merseyside supplied the majority of Harrison Line officers and crew.*

Around-the-clock working is a feature of all modern ports and Liverpool is no exception. The need for vessels to arrive on one tidal window and sail on the next is paramount for maintaining schedules. Here, a Hapag-Lloyd container vessel is almost ready to depart, the final containers being positioned by straddle carrier to the container crane at the forward end of the vessel.

In the summer of 1992 Liverpool played host to the tall ships, a collection of sailing boats from many countries around the world, and they were berthed at every possible quayside in both Liverpool and Birkenhead. Thousands of spectators lined both sides of the river for the parade of sail when the visiting tall ships left the river. Pictured is a Spanish boat leaving the river followed by a Russian tall ship.

The Liverpool waterfront had taken on a new look in this early 1990s picture of the famous 'three graces' of the Liver Building, the Cunard Building and the Port of Liverpool Building pictured from Canning Dock.

CHAPTER SEVEN

Mersey Tugs

The majority of vessels using the Mersey River are assisted to and from their berths by tugs. These powerful workhorses are operated by two major companies. The Alexandra Towing Co. was formed in 1887, taking over tug companies dating back over 150 years. It is now called Adsteam Towage and is owned by Adsteam Marine, formerly the Adelaide Steam Ship Co. Ltd. The other major force on the river is Svitzer–Marine Ltd, formerly Cory Towage, but probably best known as Rea Towing Co. Ltd.

Pictured in the late 1970s in Royal Seaforth is the former Lamey tug Hornby, *now in the Alexandra Towing Co. fleet, manoeuvring the bulk carrier* World Argus. *In the background are vessels from Manchester Liners and the ACT fleet.*

Above: *Alexandra Towing's* Nelson *pictured in Seaforth in the early 1970s, and in Hornby Dock attaching the bow rope to a general cargo vessel prior to departure.*

Left: *Sister tug to both* Nelson *and* Brocklebank *is* Langton, *pictured assisting ACL's* Atlantic Prelude *through Gladstone Lock in the early 1980s.*

Above: *Three ATCL tugs assisting a Royal Navy submarine berthing at Seaforth's S6 berth.*

Below: *Rea Towing's Eldergarth pushing amidships to an unnamed bulk carrier alongside Seaforth's S2 berth. Pictured in 1990, this new boat is bigger and more powerful than her older sister tugs ahead of the bulker.*

Viewed from the forward deck of ACL's Atlantic Crown is the ATCL tug Canada *taking the bow rope into the River Mersey.*

CHAPTER EIGHT

Liverpool's Links with Ireland

The area between Liverpool's Pier Head and Stanley Dock was known as the 'Coastwise' area as it handled short sea and passenger traffic predominantly to and from Ireland. Coast Lines (latterly P&O Ferries) ran the nightly sailings to Belfast with the B&I Line trading from Waterloo Dock to Dublin with a sailing in late evening. Access to these berths was from the Waterloo River Entrance. A container lift-on, lift-off service also operated from the adjacent berth.

The end of an era: the two famous 'night boats' Ulster Queen *and* Ulster Prince *pictured at South West Princes Dock after the P&O Ferries nightly service to Belfast had ended.*

The area has been extensively redeveloped to include an hotel and office accommodation, maintaining the water theme with a shallower dock that is also narrower than the original working Princes Dock.

In July 1981 B&I Line's *Leinster* made her maiden voyage to Liverpool. Her sister vessel *Connacht* sailed from Waterloo Dock on the lunchtime sailing (summer schedule) and saluted the new build as she arrived in mid river.

Left: Connacht *manoeuvring stern-first into the river prior to swinging into position on the far side of the channel.*

Below left: *The two 'sisters' passing. The* Leinster *is dressed overall.*

Below: *A close up of the port side of the new* Leinster.

Above: *The last of the previous generation of B&I Passenger/Freight vessels,* Innisfallen *is pictured alongside the Brocklebank Terminal that was brought into use for B&I vessels after the Waterloo Dock River entrance was closed due to the high cost of maintenance and the lack of regular traffic.*

Below: *As the passenger ferries ended they were replaced with a new breed of vessel – the roll-on, roll-off ferry – with all the cargo on wheels. A lot of these units would be accompanied by the haulage tractor unit whose driver would accompany the load to its final destination. Other units would be hauled by tractor unit onto the vessel then secured for the crossing to be hauled off at the port of discharge to await a local haulier to complete delivery. This P&O Company/B&I Line joint service would be known as PANDORO (P&O Roll On, Roll Off). Pictured at the Gladstone No.3 berth is the* Viking Trader, *typical of the vessels used on these services between Liverpool/Belfast and Dublin. This type of vessel has three trailer decks including the weather (open) deck and two covered decks. The three-storey sheds of North Two Gladstone were demolished to make space available for the secure parking of trailers.*

    The former offices for HM Customs at the east end of the berth are still visible, as are the offices at the east end of South Two Gladstone. Both premises have since been demolished.

Belfast Car Ferries. Belfast-Liverpool-Belfast

Opposite:

Above: *With P&O Ferries concentrating on freight vessels, a passenger vessel supplied by Belfast Car Ferries commenced operation in June 1982, sailing between Liverpool and Belfast and carrying a mix of freight, passengers and trade cars.* St Colum I *operated from a berth never previously used in Langton Dock. With her bow to the north, the starboard side of the vessel was along the infilled site of the Langton Graving docks and Langton Branch Dock. The former transit shed for Langton Branch Dock was used for passenger car marshalling prior to boarding. The arrival time was 7a.m. with departure at 11a.m. the same day.*

An original 'company issue' postcard of St Colum I *at sea and another view of her pictured alongside her Langton Dock berth.*

Below: *After B&I Line departed from the passenger scene, several other operators provided services to Dublin, none of which lasted very long. Pictured in Langton Lock is Sealink British Ferries'* Earl William *prior to docking at North Brocklebank Branch Dock. This service operated seven days each week, with arrivals at 6p.m. each evening and departure at 10.30p.m.*

This page:

Another link with Dublin was the short-lived company Dublin Ferries. Operating from the West Alexandra Dock, this two-vessel operation was essentially a freight service with containers loaded to mafi trailers (a dock/ship-use only trailer).

These two views are of the East German-flagged Gleichberg *alongside her berth.*

Above: *The second vessel in service for Dublin Ferries was* City of Dublin, *pictured underway in the dock.*

Below: *Another regular sailing to and from Liverpool was the Isle of Man Steam Packet roll-on, roll-off vessel* Peveril, *operating between Hornby Dock and Douglas, Isle of Man. This freight-only service operated weekday evenings with arrivals and departures some three hours apart. Here,* Peveril *is pictured in mid-river as she 'swings' inwards towards Gladstone Lock.*

CHAPTER NINE

The 1990s in the Modern Port of Liverpool

Cunard Line celebrated its 150th anniversary in July 1990 and to mark the occasion the cruise liner *Queen Elizabeth 2* arrived in the Mersey River on 24 July 1990. On the previous tide the *Atlantic Conveyor*, part of the ACL fleet, but managed by Cunard Line, had docked at her regular berth of S3 Royal Seaforth Container Terminal. Many thousands of spectators flocked to the riverside to get the best views as QE2 passed Crosby inward just before 11a.m. with a flotilla of small craft waiting to join the run up river towards her anchorage south of the Pier Head Landing Stage.

Tugs from The Alexandra Towing Co. took her ropes just before Seaforth rocks and stood by until late in the evening. With a firework display in mid-river prior to her 10p.m. departure, most Merseysiders witnessed a memorable event. With the decline in passenger traffic, the Port has only had limited cruise ships visiting since, with most having to lock into the dock system in order for passenger boarding and transfer.

The Princes Dock area was under consideration for future development as a site for offices and an hotel now that the quaysides were no longer handling vessels. Waterloo River entrance was also closed to vessels with any remaining traffic moving north towards the more modern docks, and the conversion of the former Waterloo grain warehouse adjacent the Dock Road into luxury flats and apartments was completed.

The Port Authority, The Mersey Docks & Harbour Co., moved from its prestigious waterfront offices to a purpose-built complex at the entrance to Seaforth Dock. Originally planned for the opening of Seaforth, this office building finally arrived some thirty years after it was first planned.

The Freeport continued to grow. The status of Freeport was given to a large area of the north docks including Seaforth several years earlier. This enabled traders to hold cargo within warehouses in the Freeport without paying VAT until the goods were sold on and moved out.

Changes in shipping trends saw several new customers move and return as the Port's fortunes continued to grow. Gracechurch Container Line, part of the Borchard Line, moved the short sea trade from Garston to Seaforth when access to a berth would be available at any state of the tide.

General cargo, in decline for many years, had a major boost with new services using the old quays at Vittoria Dock, Birkenhead, after a break of eight years. Trades included timber, steel and specialist heavy lift cargoes for delivery via the M53 motorway link.

The ending of the National Dock Labour Scheme in 1989 had seen several new trades arrive within the Port, including large coal imports to the quaysides of S2 Gladstone prior to the specialist Powergen Plant being built at S1 Gladstone Dock.

Scrap metals continued to cover the once busy quaysides from Seaforth to Huskisson, with several companies operating bulk carriers loading scrap metals. Imports of Scottish granite became a feature of Seaforth's S10 berth, the granite being shipped in bulk carriers from Glensanda Quarry at Loch Linnhe in Scotland for road building in the north-west region. This product would be discharged to the open quayside by conveyor direct from the vessel and moved by pay loader to the adjacent site north of her berth.

Imports of Canadian newsprint to both sides of the river, at Seaforth's S7 berth and Birkenhead's Vittoria Dock, continued with the use of a variety of specialist ships, including some with side ramps to prevent paper damages during loading and unloading.

Short sea roll-on, roll-off traffic started to move back to Liverpool and a new company, Norse Irish Ferries, introduced a

Above: *The QE2 arriving in the River Mersey, passing Perch Rock, New Brighton.*

Below: *Turning on the tide with Tug* Canada *assisting.*

daily freight service between North Brocklebank Dock and Victoria Terminal 2 in Belfast. This complemented the P&O (Pandoro) service to Dublin from Gladstone Dock. The container links provided by Coastal Containers Limited between Seaforth's S6 berth and Belfast started the development of links to Dublin for lift-on, lift-off containers.

Above: *The QE2 late evening, prior to sailing.*

Below: *Anchored in mid-river.*

Above: Norse Lagan *loading at night.*

Below: *Liverpool's shipping connections with Russia have long-standing traditions, including trade with the Latvian port of Riga. This trade was maintained by a multi-purpose roll-on, roll-off container vessel capable of handling a variety of containerised cargo and vehicles. Pictured here is* Inhenzer Kreylis *at Seaforth.*

Extensions to the Freightliner rail connection at Seaforth doubled its size and opened up a Euro Rail link with the Channel Tunnel. This was for container swap bodies as well as containers, offering fast transit times from Liverpool to Paris (15 hours), Strasbourg (18 hours) and Milan (36 hours).

September 1993 saw the opening of the Powergen coal terminal at S1 Gladstone Dock. This terminal, equipped with two ship-to-shore bulk grab cranes, handled coal at a rate of 25,000 tons per day. With storage of up to 325,000 tons to the south of the quay on land between Gladstone and

Hornby Dock, a rail link was re-established to load direct to rail wagons en route to Fiddlers Ferry Power Station near Warrington. Pictured on the left is a Powergen Bulk Carrier prior to arrival, and on the right, discharging coal at the terminal.

Offshore supply vessels started to use the port, supplying the rigs of the Liverpool Bay field with both stores and personnel. For the period between 1991 and 1998 The Mersey Docks & Harbour Co. achieved record turnover and profits. Throughput tonnages grew from 24.7 million to 33 million. Company turnover increased from £69.5 million to £179.7 million.

Profits increased from £13.2 million to £47.6 million.

ACL G3 vessel Atlantic Concert *is pictured alongside S3 berth Royal Seaforth Container Terminal*

Andrew Weir Shipping charter vessel City of Liverpool *loading containers during the night at Royal Seaforth's S5 berth.*

Mersey Docks and Harbour Company Property Developments

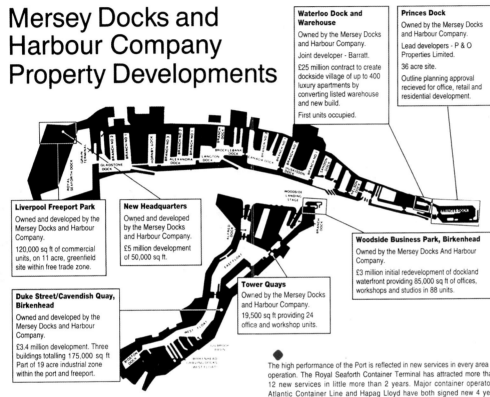

Waterloo Dock and Warehouse

Owned by the Mersey Docks and Harbour Company.

Joint developer - Barratt.

£25 million contract to create dockside village of up to 400 luxury apartments by converting listed warehouse and new build.

First units occupied.

Princes Dock

Owned by the Mersey Docks and Harbour Company.

Lead developers - P & O Properties Limited.

36 acre site.

Outline planning approval recieved for office, retail and residential development.

Liverpool Freeport Park

Owned and developed by the Mersey Docks and Harbour Company.

120,000 sq ft of commercial units, on 11 acre, greenfield site within free trade zone.

New Headquarters

Owned and developed by the Mersey Docks and Harbour Company.

£5 million development of 50,000 sq ft.

Duke Street/Cavendish Quay, Birkenhead

Owned and developed by the Mersey Docks and Harbour Company.

£3.4 million development. Three buildings totalling 175,000 sq ft. Part of 19 acre industrial zone within the port and freeport.

Tower Quays

Owned by the Mersey Docks and Harbour Company.

19,500 sq ft providing 24 office and workshop units.

Woodside Business Park, Birkenhead

Owned by the Mersey Docks And Harbour Company.

£3 million initial redevelopment of dockland waterfront providing 85,000 sq ft of offices, workshops and studios in 88 units.

Containers through the Port in 1992 totalled a record 335,000 teus (20ft equivalent units) compared with 289,000 teus in 1991. Timber and Forest Products rose to 791,000 tonnes (612,000 tonnes); Grain and animal feed 2,020,000 tonnes (1,983,000 tonnes); Bulk liquids 1,798,000 tonnes (915,000 tonnes); Other Bulks 3,289,000 tonnes (3,267,000 tonnes); Tranmere Oil Terminal 12,244,000 tonnes (11,572,000 tonnes); General Cargo 470,000 tonnes (372,000 tonnes).

Liverpool is now handling similar annual volumes of cargo as in the 1950s and '60s, regarded by many as the post war "heyday" of the Port. But in the '50s and '60s as many as 14,000 port operations workers were employed to discharge and load the cargoes. Today, the Port of Liverpool employs some 400.

The high performance of the Port is reflected in new services in every area of operation. The Royal Seaforth Container Terminal has attracted more than 12 new services in little more than 2 years. Major container operators Atlantic Container Line and Hapag Lloyd have both signed new 4 year contracts with the Port for their joint North Atlantic service. Moreline has established several container services at the Royal Seaforth Terminal including Balt Canada Line to Montreal, Besta Line to East Africa and the Latvian service to Riga.

Other services to move to the Terminal from other ports in the last two years include the Coastal Container Line daily service to Belfast, Gracechurch, Borchard, Ellerman and Zim Line services to the Mediterranean, MACPAK's weekly service to Spain, the Ellerman services to Portugal, Railfreight Distribution's daily services to Northern and Southern Ireland and the Delmas service to West Africa.

Expansion in the number of shipping services to the Mediterranean, Europe and Ireland has enabled Liverpool to develop as a hub port providing the fastest transhipment of cargoes moving on North Atlantic deep sea services.

Liverpool is the major Port for trade between the UK and Ireland. Daily roll-on roll-off and lift-on lift-off shipping services to Belfast and Dublin handle 2.5 million tonnes of trade each year - almost 30% of all freight crossing the Irish Sea, Liverpool moves 60% of all unitised traffic between the Republic of Ireland and the UK. It is the only British port on the Irish Sea serving both Northern and Southern Ireland and the only UK port providing Irish trade with direct deepsea and nearsea transhipment to vital world markets such as North America and the Mediterranean. As the only Irish Sea port with a designated Channel Tunnel Euro Rail Terminal for unitised cargo, it is the only location to provide a landbridge for trade to and from Ireland, the UK and Europe via the Chunnel.

When the Channel Tunnel opens at the end of 1993 Irish Sea trade will share space on trains moving between the Port of Liverpool Euro Rail Terminal and Europe, with domestic traffic generated in and destined for the North West Region of England and containers transferred from North Atlantic shipping services. More than £1 million has been spent by the Mersey Docks and Harbour Company on expanding the rail terminal to cope with increased volume. Indicative transit times for freight moving between the Port of Liverpool Euro Rail Terminal and major European centres via the Channel Tunnel - Liverpool to Paris 15 hours, Frankfurt 28 hours, Milan 32 hours.

In 1991 the Mersey Docks and Harbour Company acquired the successful Coastal Container Line, enabling control of terminal operations at both ends of the route and further developing the Port of Liverpool's trade with Ireland through the Irish Sea central corridor. Coastal has since opened a terminal at Dublin Port for its own Liverpool - Dublin service launched early in 1993 and for other services.

Liverpool's geographic location at the centre of the United Kingdom's motorway network, is also gaining renewed recognition as an important economic advantage to shippers. Companies, under recessionary pressures to review total transportation costs, are becoming increasingly aware of the inland haulage savings to be gained from serving major industrial areas from Liverpool - a factor which will have even greater significance in 1994 when new EC regulations are introduced restricting the speed of commercial vehicles to a maximum of 56mph.

Liverpool has trading links with practically every part of the world by more than 60 international shipping services. Liverpool is the major UK port for trade with the Eastern Seaboard of North America and is among Britain's top five container ports. Liverpool imports more grain than any other UK port, exports over a million tonnes of scrap metal a year, and is one of the major UK ports for timber and forest products and edible oils and fats.

Liverpool is also an increasingly significant import port for low sulphur fossil fuels for the power generating industry. A new £40 million environmentally sensitive bulk terminal is being developed by PowerGen at Gladstone Dock to handle up to 5 million tonnes of coal a year, mainly for onward rail movement to Fiddler's Ferry Power Station. Liverpool has also developed a bulk liquid terminal for a new fuel traffic, Orimulsion from Venezuela.

The Mersey Docks & Harbour Co. 'factfile' 1993.

FREEPORT

The Mersey Docks and Harbour Company owns and operates Liverpool Freeport, superimposed upon more than 800 acres (320 hectares) of the Port of Liverpool on both banks of the Mersey.

◆

Liverpool Freeport handles £5 million worth of goods a week for hundreds of companies serving over 80 countries. Since opening in November 1984, it has handled £3 billion worth of traffic. More than 1 million sq ft (100,000 sq m) of property is occupied by warehousing, processing and manufacturing companies. Nearly 1 million sq ft more will be available with the 70 acre expansion of the Freeport and Port area. Liverpool Freeport Park provides 120,000 sq ft (11,152 sq metres) of state of the art warehousing for a range of companies serving the UK and wider markets with computers, food processing equipment, and high-value excise goods. Among the latest companies to locate in the free zone is the world's largest manufacturer of fancy dress, based in New York. Express Cargo Forwarding, a division of Ireland's biggest logistics company, has taken up 50,000 sq. ft of warehousing space in the flagship development of Liverpool Intermodal Freeport Terminal, doubling the company's accomodation in Liverpool Freeport.

◆

Liverpool Freeport has Britain's first operational freight village, located alongside the designated Euro Rail Terminal for Channel Tunnel freight - one of only 9 in the UK and the first private sector operated terminal for both Channel Tunnel and domestic freight services. The zone offers freedom from Import Duty, Import VAT, EU levies and quotas.

◆

Mersey Docks used the knowledge acquired in the development of Liverpool Freeport, to launch Medway Freeport in 1994 , which is initially focused upon the 283 acres (114.5 hectares) of the Port of Sheerness.

OVERSEAS CONSULTANCY

The expertise of the Mersey Docks and Harbour Company is applied in many parts of the world through Portia Management Services, the international arm of the Port of Liverpool and the UK's largest and longest established port management and consultancy organisation. Portia is currently undertaking a $155 million, 12 year contract upgrading and operating the major private port of San Nicolas in Argentina and is involved in the development of a new grain handling facility in Mombasa. Other countries where Portia is carrying out consultancy projects include the People's Republic of China, Vietnam, Kuwait, Bahrain, Poland, United Arab Emirates, Nigeria, Bulgaria and Pakistan. It is currently bidding for additional contracts in Africa, South America and other parts of the world.

The Mersey Docks and Harbour Company
Directors and Executive Management

G. H. Waddell	Chairman	D. Crampton	Director of Medway
P.T. Furlong	Managing Director and Chief Executive	A.J.W.D. Don	Director of Planning
		A.I. Findlay	Finance Director
P.A. Jones	Deputy Chief Executive and Port Operations Director	F.Robotham	Director of Marketing
		F. W. Taylor	Non executive
A.V. Allen	Non executive	K.J. Wharton	Shipping and Overseas Development Director
S.A.Bird	Commercial Director		
W.J. Bowley	Director of Legal Services and Company Secretary	T.D. Williams	Director of Estates

The Mersey Docks and Harbour Company sites on the Internet are:
Port of Liverpool website address: www.merseydocks.co.uk
Medway Ports website address: www.medwayports.com

THE MERSEY DOCKS AND HARBOUR COMPANY
Contact: The Marketing Department or the Public Relations Department,
The Mersey Docks and Harbour Company, Maritime Centre,
Port of Liverpool L21 1LA. Tel: 0151-949 6000 Fax: 0151-949 6338

THE MERSEY DOCKS AND HARBOUR COMPANY

FACT FILE

Spring 1999

INTRODUCTION

The Mersey Docks and Harbour Company, ranked among the Top 250 U.K. companies, owns and operates the Port of Liverpool and the Medway Ports of Sheerness and Chatham.

◆

With Liverpool located on the West Coast and Medway on the South East Coast of Britain, the Mersey Group of ports - the second largest in the country - is strongly placed to offer shippers and shipowners comprehensive coverage of the United Kingdom. Together, the ports handle 33 million tonnes of cargo a year.

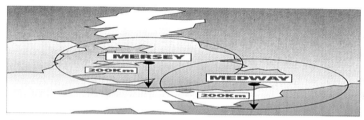

Liverpool is one of the United Kingdom's largest and most successful ports. It is also one of Britain's most comprehensive in the range of ships and cargoes it handles.

◆

Medway Ports provide the highest calibre of service in a range of niche trades and are market leaders in Britain's fruit and trade vehicle movements. Sheerness was the first major UK port to achieve BS5750 quality accreditation and subsequently achieved ISO 9002 re-accreditation.

◆

The Mersey Docks and Harbour Company achieved record turnover and profits in 1998. Operating profit from continuing activities at £53.3 million rose 11% compared with 1997. Group turnover increased by 6.6% over the previous year, to £179.7 million. Profit before tax rose to £47.6 million in 1998 against £34.6 million the year before. At the Port of Liverpool, container traffic rose from 460,000 TEUs (Twenty Foot Equivalent Units) in 1997 to 487,000 TEUs in 1998. Roll-on roll-off volumes increased by 15.8% and passenger numbers grew by 54.5% to 581,000. The Port of Liverpool handled a total of 30,300,000 tonnes in 1998 (1997: 30,800,000 tonnes). Cargo moving through Medway Ports totalled 2,700,000 tonnes (1997: 2,600,000 tonnes) with Chatham Docks exceeding 1,000,000 tonnes for the first time.

TRADING PERFORMANCE
Recent trading performances of the Mersey Docks and Harbour Company:

	1991	1992	1993	1994	1995	1996	1997	1998
Throughput (tonnes m)	24.7	27.8	29.3	31.3	31.9	33.0	33.4	33.0
Turnover (£m)	£69.5	£86.4	£98.4	£129.9	£138	£149.7	£168.5	£179.7
Profit (£m)	£13.2	£15.2	£20.9	£33.6	£31.7	£29.7	£34.6	£47.6
Dividend per share	6.00p	7.5p	9.00p	10.5p	11.50p	12.75p	14.50p	16.00p
Earnings per share	17.00p	15.05p	19.96p	25.33p	24.48p	22.77p	27.56p	38.30p
Net Assets (£m)	£118.7	£124.1	£150.2	£164.3	£170.9	£238.8	£252.2	£272.8

ATLANTIC CONTAINER LINE

www.ACLcargo.com

Opposite: *The Mersey Docks & Harbour Co. 'factfile' 1999.*

Above: *An ACL postcard of a G3 vessel* Cutaway.

Below: *A 1987 map of the Port of Liverpool.*

Overleaf: *Liverpool Docks from the air.*

If you are interested in purchasing other books published by Tempus,
or in case you have difficulty finding any Tempus books in your local bookshop,
you can also place orders directly through our website

www.tempus-publishing.com

or from

BOOKPOST, Freepost, PO Box 29, Douglas, Isle of Man IM99 1BQ
Tel 01624 836000   email bookshop@enterprise.net